I wanted to kill myself while in the process of writing this book.

Who am I?

No matter what my government name is
That is still not who I am
To some I'm too skinny
Others I'm too short
To God I am him
What's my calling
I try to live in the now
But instead I find myself lost
Salty tears that slides
Down this oily brown face
The pain that couldn't be erased
Has taken my body hostage
In need of a revelation
To find out who am I
Whether it be in life or death
~~WhatI~~ What I am isn't who I am

Collarbones and Bruises

In my poems
~~Wherel~~ Where I spill my feelings
Wrapped with love
Dipped in sorrows
Sliced with the knife of pain
Salty tears dried out my skin
Biting into the words
Filling my insides with trash
This is bad for my health
But it's the only food I have
Besides the dessert of lies
Left by my past experiences
A sinner lips
With thoughts of
Love in your mental
Softly fingers caressing
My collarbone
Placing a spell on each shoulder
Leaving weakness in my body
Opening up the wounds

Death to the present me

16:

You scratch my back
I pull your hair
It's steamy
We sweating
My name
You scream it
Your love
I stamp it
You're cumming
I'm nutting
Love

Sinful Hope

She missed her period
Nervous and in fear
Of what her mother
Will say, she disappears
Left a note that said

[Hope was here]

Faded petals

Stain spill on thy flower (body)
Damaging the petals
Leaving red marks all over

~~Amother's~~ A Mother's ~~touch~~Touch

Her kisses bringeth warm
The love being transferred
There for your pain
outsiders give
heal your sickness
making you feel better
feeding the tummy
so there will be no starvation
preparing your brain for life
there for you whenever you call
her heart feels your hurt
when there is damage inside of you
mama's going to be there
one of the few who will still be
even after everyone else has left
a queen with love and strength
it warms your heart to see her smile
saddens you to see her frown
her presence brings energy no other can bring
the simple touch of a mother

lovers in a park

every walk becomes a mile
a bond we made
with love that will never fade
a promise worth while

holding hands
our first time around
the silent peaceful sound
mother sun at a stands

beautiful smells in the air
the cool breeze rubbing against us
with no sign of dust
no others being there

Mother Nature looking on
giving her a good show
nudist in a park spilling art
you and nature is all one needs

the unspoken truth

as il lay here in silence
il try to find what it is
that life really wants from me
listening hard, to hear the sounds
not just any sound
the sound of life
the stars, crickets, wind, trees
it's night fall and everyone's
sleeping
inside my brain
there's a loud party going on
with my thoughts dj'ing
my feelings dancing
il ask not verbally but emotionally
what's my purpose
my reason my calling
maybe il have wasted time
asking
the ticking from my clock
the tapping clicking from my phone
afraid to surf the internet
because their lives may be better than mine
il don't understand
but thethen again, who does

not your average love letter.

dear you who fucked me over
you said forever
i~~l~~ guess that was ~~aparta~~ a part of your lies
but it's all kosher
you left when things got tough
without so much of a warning
i~~l~~ should've seen this coming
blinded by love now ~~iml~~ I'm mourning
it hurts to know we were so close
to now becoming so far
leaving me with mental and physical war
the ~~saddens~~ sadness that runs through my veins now
good ~~perf romance~~ performance, take a bow

sincerely, the hurt one

Wondering blue jay

~~sometimes~~Sometimes it hurts to know, but it is the only ~~way.i~~way. I can
see the pain that hides inside of you. ~~we~~We are all artist just painting our
lives. ~~the~~The beginnings of an idea.
~~my~~My naked skin finds
fault in touching yet and all she thinks that he'll be with her forever.

~~ponder~~Ponder on this

addicted.

darling ~~i~~I, so thankful
you grace me with
~~your~~you're special
and since ~~i~~I fell in love
(I'm over thinking)

writing poetry
try~~ing to~~na keep mind at ease
reading books
~~tryna~~trying to increase my vocabulary
you see me choking
off your fucking love
but you still haven't came
to help me cough it up
undressing you with my eyes
and fucking you with my mind
you cut me open
and left me there
until ~~i~~I dried out
~~i~~I don't believe the people ~~i~~I meet
for the people ~~i~~I meet always leave me to be
a black victim
found lying on the floor
overdosed, the reason
addiction

her.

~~i've~~I've never met you
but I know you're out there
from every smell to every touch
~~i~~I can feel your presence
through the air
the night time falls and my thinking begins
~~laying~~lying next to an empty space letting this love sink in
gripping the sheets and rubbing my body
visualizing your naked soul connecting with my body
closing my eyes and biting my lips
grabbing your waist and squeezing your hips
please don't let this end
if it does, ~~i~~I wouldn't know where to begin

a worth of ~~realzation~~realization:

she opened her legs to a guy she barely knows
giving her priceless temple
to him who has slept with many hoes
yet she falls for the guy
thinking he will change
with experience that became a lie
now she wants an exchange
after being drug through the dirt
of heartbreaks and cold lies
she finally realize her worth
never to again be fooled
by the eyes of love
but to overruled
her feelings and think above

tears of a poor man

feet like stone
hands of wood
another day of starvation
and suffering from dehydration

old raggedy rugs
dark skin and ashy knuckles
everyday his faith is being tested
but he tries to remain calm and be patient

this is beginning to be too common
not even love to share with a woman
il feel death coming closer
if this is true, dear God get it over

sleepless.

coloring with a white crayon
on white paper
strap to these sheets
falling deeply
into this spell called sleep
a place il visit often
where my dreams are now reality
to think doesn't hurt my brain
no matter the thoughts
il have no idea
what I'm writing about
letting my thoughts
ride the midnight wave
knowing once il awake
il won't remember this place

sounds of silence

tape rolling
sewing machines running
humming from an old man
squeaky shoes from a long stand
tapping foot petals
the clashing of metals
cracking bones
and aching moans
anger in the belly
the need for food most definitely
Is it time yet

8 to 5

writing in my notepad
at this fucking 8-5
I'm getting tired of this shit
man il want to live my life
be free
and do me
lately I've been on some other shit
following the path of others is not
relevant
man forget this, il quit

overdosed.

inhaling in the sadness
scrapping off the pain
~~tryna~~trying to stop madness
as ~~i~~I watch it rain
fighting back the tears
depression here

shooting up with drugs
the feeling got me high
but this drug called love
so it'll be alright
if it's like this
~~i~~I don't want ~~no~~ any part of it

your words full of
broken promises and lies
that filled me up
with the hope of forever
lingering inside of me
ohh the agony

find.

to be alone in a world
where ~~il~~ lose humans
and connect with nature
the physical me they see
inside is where ~~il~~ scream
shouting for a responder
drowning at the lower
end of my stomach
climbing to my ribs
to reach the top
but ~~i'm~~I'm steady falling
someone please, help me out

poetry

you listen when il have much to say
holding my every thought inside your heart
even when il leave you
you always let me back in
my the patience that you hold within
my tears dripped on you
smearing your skin
you've seen my hurt
you heard my cry
no ink was wasted
when il wrote on your body
my silence sung
and you let it
my fellow humans couldn't understand
the relationship that we hold
wrapped my treasures inside you
hidden deep within
spilled love all over you
watching as you soak it all in
though my flesh is doing all the movement
my spirit is releasing all the talking
while my soul is peeling itself
out of my skin to lay down my truths between these healing wounds
your body catches my pain, my joy, my life
you open me up and turn me inside out
this love affair has gone on long enough
letslet's lock fingers and never let go
il tell my friends about you
they all would like to meet you
Someday my dear, the world
will hear from you until then,
stay true

Thursday

it's morning
the voice of God awakens me
il rise to the fresh scent of love
with you on my mind and life in my heart
sounds of morning cruising through my earlobes
the happiness that comes from receiving your good morning text
it creates a smile that only a baby would understand
the flowers are blooming
the sun is shining
il give you a gift
just cause it's Thursday

nightly thoughts:

Someone once ask me
~~what~~What do I want to be in life
I once had an answer
Now, it's a different story
I'm a lost child who has to get on board and fast
I can't keep making the same mistakes that I made in the past
Things can change so quickly
Nowadays, you have to think more clearly
No one trust anymore and people are losing their patience with love
Seems to me like everyone's giving up
I over think a lot more now
More than I should somehow
I think I'm becoming the person I want to be and losing the old me
While everyone's sleeping well
I'm up thinking... Wish me well

Words ~~From~~from ~~A~~a Junkie:

Keep hope alive
Never let it die
Life has many choices
Just be wise
Time can be your
Friend or enemy
Just know, it doesn't wait
For you or me
Things get tough
~~Ppl~~ People become strangers
Just keep praying
God & Jesus are your trainers
When you have free time
Do something ~~Positive~~positive
It's way better than
Thinking of something negative
May not have much money
But ~~You~~ you have much love
You may say that's nothing
But that's a blessing from above
Music to my body
Poetry to my soul
Up lifting spirits
My heart continues to grow
Nothing but the clothes on my back
A pen & a pad
Making dumb wishes
For things I never had
Life sucked the
life out of me
Now here ~~i~~I am
Sad and lonely

old habits:

Someone once told me, I could be anything I want to be if I just put my mind to it
Add my heart, soul, and dedication I'll be fine through it
But who knows where it might goes so I'm blind to it
My life is full of bad choices where I should've thought smarter
Not worrying ~~bout~~about consequences
Too busy living for the moment
I know I know... Young dumb, ~~right ...~~right... Yeah
Wish I could just visit stars for one night
Seems like they the only ones who listen when I tell 'em my vision
A kid with bad teeth ~~who's~~whose parents was split separated
Dang~~.~~...
Got caught up in the moment
Like hobo on the corner
Man it's sad to see 'em homeless
It's time to make a change
Starting with myself, building on the old me so kisses to the remains

the flower that never got pick

never plucked
rarely touch
ran over
no one notice
but still you shine
one of a kind
the wind blew you
God created you
gaining energy from the sun
now il see the truth
It is you my love
Grow and blossom
Into what you was made to be

broken thoughts

how could you steal my thoughts without even asking or trading something in return~~.~~....type this with your eyelash. detach yourself from everything. my appetite for love. if i̶l cut you open, flowers will fall out. lay your spirit down. thigh ~~gap.dash~~gap. dash yourself with a bucket of poetry. ..was i̶l just another i̶l can hear your heart screaming. you took everything but my bones. just randomly converse with outsiders you don't know. (dissatisfaction) ~~climb~~climbs inside my head and tell your theories about the universe. the day when our eyes first met~~.~~....everyone's a serial killer inside their head. ..are you poor in knowledge, money, or ~~wisdom.~~wisdom?

words left unsaid

would you believe me
if il told you
that the girl who I'm writing about
in this poem was you
or would you overlook that too
il was hoping you would call
but you never did
wrote you many texts
no response at all
though the atmosphere
is filled with negative energy
i'mI'm walking on the land of love
hoping to reach you
il guess this really is the end for us
sigh, il hope you're doing better than il am

stale love
splashes of abstract feelings
thrown on the wall
painting a picture
of this beautiful soul
weeping cries through the night
scars of her past appears
spilling emotions on her pillow
she squeezes the sheets
only to realize her loneliness
the cold atmosphere
breezes through the room
as her bones lock up
thoughts begin to rumble
how could this happen
giving her treasures to a man
where in the end
left the scene with no feelings
she cuts through her heart
with a dagger
that spelled hate on it
blood of feelings poured out
she picks up the emotion
that said love
releases it from the hand
landing it on it back into pieces
those love songs weren't just love songs anymore
meaning came with them
and so did pain
open wounds no stitches
a positive being came into her life
afraid to open up
hiding her feelings
she drops them into the deepest sea
where sharks of trust, faithfulness, honesty swum
no man shall seek in survive
though, he dive to swim
a tough quest with no path
lower vibrations
peaceful meditation
beneath the sea
he soon reached
when ~~suddenly~~ ...suddenly... to be continued

broken strangers

lust grace my eyes
as il first lay sight on her
the pain spilling from her heart
open wounds with no stitches
viewing the sorrows she lay down
building up momentum to speak
but afraid of the response
so il remain silent and in peace
hoping to connect
with the inner being
courage grew inside of me
hello, this word il finally release
conversing on and on
her ~~tone sing~~tone sings to my ears
soft and gentle
each word filled with love
high vibes positive energy
flowing through the wave sound
over the phone
two hearts with cracks in them
the fear of opening again
should we stop now or keep going

torn into pieces:

il wish that il could pause life for a sec to catch my breath.
one minute my mother was telling me you don't want to grow up too fast.
the next minute il was grown and feeling alone. things got tough. il begin to
think it really wasn't luck that kept me sane all those years. now that il am
older and il see for myself, life is something. that something we all search
for. that something that can't be determined in one lifetime.

insult:

i̶l never cared for
that sad girl
whose love was
only shown to grasp
my attention
sour words left her lips
i̶l knew then she was poisonous

moon:

it gets lonely up here
the few friends il have
only hangs around during
the night no one to come
and meet me
visualizing how it be
to have others live with me
every so often, they examine
my life here
that's about it
maybe someday, that'll all change

my lovers gone:

while my hair was still tangled
you came on a white horse
with peaches in your hands
smelling like the ol' picking field
where the soil was still wet
il locked my fingers into yours
throwing myself on to you
tasting your lips gripping your hips
messy sheets lie underneath
round 3 before your flee

afraid

afraid to tell you
that if il told you
you wouldn't understand
judge me then leave me
like the other earthlings
that came and went
taking what they can
bit by bit
off my body
or what's left of it
il could hear the anger
roaring up inside your tone
knowing then
you didn't understand
feeling hopeless x all alone (x means & ?)

my letter to you:

    this is my letter to you
il hope that you will get this
letting you know il miss you
  iHII'll be waiting for that kiss

   for now il can only dream
  of the things il would do
  leave your window open
one day iHII'll be coming through

postcard:

blood leaking
from the skin
cracked ribs

the war isn't over
just the romance
rest in peace

no return:

mom says poppa will be back soon
but that's hard to believe
i~~l~~ heard screaming the night before
as the rain tapped my window
lighting flashing behind the trees
he left a note on my bedside
~~saying(~~saying (gone for awhile, ~~i'lll~~I'll be back soon)
waiting patiently for his return
the darkness came
noises from the ~~neighbors~~neighbor's dog rise
i~~l~~ could taste the saltiness in my tears
as they washed along my oily face
no sign of him at all
we were suppose to play catch that day
but we never did
a week later, some man came
but it's wasn't poppa
he was tall, shaggy beard with an old smelly ~~oder~~odor that could wipe out
a plantation
but he was kind, except his eyes
they locked into me
tears from my ~~mothers~~mother's face rushed
i~~l~~ could sense the emptiness in the atmosphere
reading his lips, my poppa had been shot and pronounced dead
my heart caved in
my body separated
no not my poppa
no no no
all we had left of him
was a dollar and thirty cents
that's all he had on him the night he died

flowers x skin:

out of her roots
were flowers that
spoke the truth
deep beneath
layers x layers
no one knew
soft smooth skin
like the earths
soil when watered
this love's been altered
spells of curse
sticky veins wrapped
against my skin
squeezing me tighter
the pain's coming in
the smell of her roses
opened my nose
drugged me with dozes
aster, calla, carnation (flowers)
dead, new, old, young (skin)

drunk wise words:

so what,
let 'em judge
it's not like i̶l̶ will be here forever
i̶'m̶I'm on one liver
my lungs are cloudy
the cells in my brain are falling apart
but do they really care
no
because if they did
instead of judging
they should be helping

corner prostitute:

judges by my peers
no love from my loved ones
il go out late at night
looking for a good time
just to feel loved
charging by the minutes
hours after hours
to be called slutty names
and please these dirty manes
it's not worth it
il don't deserve this
you know il had a name once
Alexandra McQueen
was what it was
now I'm just (how much)
and a dollar sign

Edgar Simon:

she doesn't notice me
or recognize me
her voice replays late
at night into my thoughts
we speak only in my dreams
set aside an empty space
just for her if she ever comes
those water blue eyes
sandy light skin
with a watermelon fragrance
from the southern city
arise to ~~a laughter~~laughter
teens around me
~~i~~I must've fell asleep
at school in my desk
the teacher calling me
my crush is still a crush
she still doesn't notice me

bleeding thoughts

nothing but beauty of
the leaves that lay
beside me
writing under a tree of hope
contemplating on the future
of mankind and existence
speaking stories of the past
connecting it with our present
we are more than a body of
brains and organs
a soul and ~~spirit with~~spirit with beliefs
some different some the same
no matter, we should come as one
create, love and meditate as one
instead we kill, rob and destroy
man environment of changes
it's time for some healing
gather around

boat ride:

the scent from
the ocean creeping
into my system

back x fourth
we go
the rocking of the boat

a brief breeze
flows by
as il glance at the sky

the clouds sure
do look
lonely up there

by evening
the day was
light gray

~~S.W~~
S.W

niggas

like the color black that doesn't fit in the rainbow
the calling of one another from my peers
niggas trip off others calling them a nigga but they play the role of a nigga
killing each other just for a piece of dough
anyway to get it so they sell dope
taking from the next man who worked hard for it
too lazy to go out and get it on his own so he'll rather kill for it
but aren't il a nigga too
the same skin color as you
brainwashed by your peers and rappers
instead of a good introductions
you start with the word nigga

silent want

~~i've~~I've never seen her before until now
the girl that brought a smile and a hello
her scent was strong and smelled like peaches
her skin was bright and smooth like ~~reeses~~Reese's
afraid to look at her because when ~~i~~I do, my jaws locked and my ~~bones shuts~~bones shut down
she sparked a flame and ~~i~~I have no idea where she came
on the right side of me there's nature
and on the left side of me there's her
mumbling words as ~~i~~I begin to speak
but ~~i~~I don't think she heard me
so ~~i~~I remained silent and continued on to think
our flesh touched
our eyes locked to our phones
but neither knew what was to come
afraid to look at up because she'll know ~~i'm~~I'm looking and probably think that ~~i'm~~I'm crazy
but ~~i'm~~I'm really not, all I'm trying to do is turn this what if into a maybe

black boy sang

dark clouds and heavy rain
teary eyes and cold pain
black boy why don't you sang
still silence lets flash back
memories ~~thats~~that's abstract
white ~~vs~~vs. black my what a history
black boy why don't you sang
deep voices and old blues
another one hung but that's nothing new
black boy why don't you sang
a painful reality ~~i~~I wish to stay asleep
although we have come a long ways, we still don't see
black boy why don't you sang
the racial slurs and ugly choice of words
thrown out into the world
back boy why don't you sing

valentine:
roses are red
the sky is blue
il am single
and il hope you are too
il know this may sound weird
but valentines is near
il don't have long
so let me make this clear
will you be my valentine
and if your answer is yes
remain and stay mine
then il am truly blessed
but if your answer is no
then il don't want to know

unappreciated

when she's ~~laying~~lying on her back she's beautiful
but when she's not playing her part she becomes a bitch
and it hurts more coming from the lips that she loves
cause she'll give her all just to see that happiness glow from her love
she spills her sadness for him to feel where she's coming from
but he ignores her playing madden and states that she is just running her
gums... to be continued

to

to her he's her man
to his boys he's their nigga
to her quality time is a plus
to him busting a nut
to her the small things matter
to him try to get her wetter
to her long night talks is love
to him it's sleepy time
to her he's hers and only hers
to him don't trip, she's just a friend

illusion:

as you rest your legs on mine
  inside il feel a deep sigh
the moment came and so did il
  il left my thoughts in the sky
neither hungry nor thirsty for your
      love and attention
because God has blessed that
    inside of me did il mention
but il will take it as dessert if the
        offer stands
  afraid to tell her how il feel
  so il let my actions stand still
a tender kind voice that speaks to
        my heart
          here

mad max:

why do il feel this way
this pain that is roaring up inside of me
spirits fighting over my flesh
daggers inside my chest
il won't spill what I'm thinking
or how I'm feeling
they won't understand and they can't fix my spirit
tears falling as il write this
dropping and splashing on my fingers tips
the need to be alone
il crave for nature
in my thoughts il have sinned
the feeling of lust to come back in
and start again

Delphinium:

empty the thoughts of a negative person
spread them out on the table and what will you find, poison
it feeds off of anger
dark thoughts that cover the light
where the patience is low, the blood is cold, no positive air flow
underneath their garden is rooted with good seeds
but the fruits grow rotten when they're not taken care of with love
cut up memories and murderous thinking

rainy days

listening to the rain
thundering & lighting
it's rather nice
but has me thinking
it gets softer then louder
dark clouds lights off
Thank God my provider
mouth close thoughts out
a blessing I say
a blessing today

violent:

the mind tell her where to go and she goes
the heart tell her how she feels and she feels
control by her feelings
one minute she says he's no good for her
and the next he's her lover
sticking by his side
cause in the beginning she promised to always be down to ride
he cut her heart with lies
no one there to dry her eyes
looking in the mirror wishing things could be the way they used to be
time has left her and so has he
make believe stories is what she tell her friends
so she ~~hide~~hides behind the false images of what should have been
all she wanted was to be love
all he wanted was lust
but as she recalled him saying
"as long as I'm living there will always be an us"
so she cries out to the God asking for his guidance
dear Lord, if this is true, then show me but if it's not, then show me the way
out
your daughter, violent

lifeless victim:

it's deeper than skin
il can feel it in your thoughts
looking through a wormhole
sending the pain through waves
in the ocean is where you'll find my feelings lost along with my tears
they cut you deep and leave you open
without so much as a thank you, you leave
locking myself alone in an abandon building
12 years later they find the bones of a missing human
to say why he did it
only one knows
dressed in all black, she comes up to the podium
opens her mouth to speak and then

"shots fired"
her body drops

...pull the trigger on your thoughts

phobia

as il release my thoughts into your juice
il hope you choke off the truth
spilling lies from your tongue
can't let my ears soak it up
injecting this art inside my veins
dark visuals replaying in the back of my mind
hoping that il never have to see the face that devoured my heart again
you lust me, used me, and left me
with words unsaid, wounds that aren't heal and time il can't get back

deep swimming

caressing your body
as il glaze your skin with warm hands and soft lips
il grab my body suit
hoping to reach the bottom of the sea
where the temperature is warmer
the water is calmer
and the treasure shall be
the deeper il swim
the louder it gets
stroke after stroke
breath after breath
il know I'm getting closer
il can feel the sweatiness
beneath my suit
my visions getting dark
and my leg muscles are beginning to cramp
then il feel something warm touch my suit
ahh, at last il have found me treasure

Natural Thoughts

random blabber
got so many dreams
~~iI wanna~~wanna be so many things
don't know where to start
~~iI~~ ask God to give me wings
you don't know what it's like to be alone
to want someone around
to be there through ups and down
~~iI~~ wrote my love in the sand
it washed away with the current
now I'm really really hurt
cause you never did see it
God on my side
evil underneath me
people lurking
the earth behind me
thinking of my next move
~~tryna tryna~~trying to make it my best move

you

in the beginning, you were just a picture
time was just something that reminded me of you
flowers, clouds, the weather too
with eyes that sparkles like the ocean when the sun's hitting it
can't seem to explain how il want to but il hope you can feel it
the vibes are wavy, the conversing is gravy
alone in a blank room, il paint a picture of you
place your skin on my lips
your collarbone is what il shoot
my imagination is all il have
now lets us ride this heavenly path...

wavering

It's not the same anymore
We used to be so much more
The conversing has gotten worse
Am I wasting my time in something that seems to be losing its worth
I lay in my bed asking God for a change
Trying to not think negative putting pressure on my brain
You tell me not to worry but your actions show me different
I don't know if this is a sign, should I listen?

past thinking

listening to voices from the past
thinking back then
il had no clue
that il would even last

some of those voices
are no longer with
myselfe and il pray for their journey
and choices

life has a funny way
of showing us
who will be here
to stay

in the present day
we rush time but when we think about it we wish it could
slow it down in a way

instead of enjoying the now
we contemplate on what's
next for us
losing sight of the now

sunset

the sun is passing
down darkness is
about to fall sounds
of the oil rigs
growing annoying to
thy ear below the
sea is a part going
on with fish mingling
crabs jamming
the end of July
is near bring on
the August hues

queen IV

your love opens me up
with a fragrance under my nose
coming into my lungs
filling them with love
touching your skin
feeling your emotions
and past memories
the pain it brings
to my fingertips
now il see why you feel
the way you do

sweaty palms

the day is almost over
sounds of the turbines
hitting the deep waves
the wind wrapping
its arms around me
with smell of old oil
what's work without hard
exhausted physically
as well as mentally
but il get an extra push
from within
carry me over
to the next day

weird voices

'tis bad
a name il dare
not speak of
fixing my mouth
to say it
but the teeth
of me bites down
on thy tongue
remembering fast
slow to speak
feelings pondering
inside of my heart

3.14
as il search the dark corners
of my mind
dusk begin to come up
from the answers underneath
waiting to tell lies
to the heart of truth
times running out
0:00

Mixed up girl

In her room
She ~~stand~~stands alone
Writing about her troubles

About the boy
She loved promised to stay
But left her for another

Tears falling
~~onto~~Onto the paper
Her voice starts to crack

She picks it up
Tears it down the middle
Who knew he would
Have her like that

Barely could breathe
Couldn't take it anymore
A bottle of pills she emptied
Pain no more

generation:

~~welcome~~Welcome to my generation
~~where~~Where brothers they dying daily
~~and~~And sisters just having babies
~~they~~They don't care about the near future

~~welcome~~Welcome to my generation
~~and~~And this my generation

Who's to say
I will live to see another day
Living in a corrupt country

Where brothers robbing brothers
Sisters backstabbing sisters

We the people of these states
Are suppose to be united
But yet we're divided

In a world where
~~there~~There is much chaos
But humans are creating it
Not Mother Earth

My generation of females
Uses words like bitch x hoes
Instead of queens x madam

The younger they come
The quicker they leave
Generation after generation
Dear God save us please

drifty thoughts

as il sit in silence
wondering what the
other side of the world
is doing, my brain
begins to drift
away from the now
into the future
who will remain
and what will go
time has shown me
nothing is forever
though we say it
it comes apart sometimes
on a different path than
the others, my route
isn't the same
holding on to God's
word, believing
hoping and praying
sigh,
il hope someday il may
find my purpose
and until il do
il will keep on seeking

room 108

Boom, crrrk, bow
Glass falling people yelling
Punches are thrown

As she lay there in tears
She doesn't feel safe
~~calling~~Calling the police terrified that they may ~~doing~~do nothing and it's
only ~~gonna~~going to make it worse

Her body is in pain her trust is out the window
Laying there covered in blood
Scratches, bruises, and torn clothes.

A gun she buys for her troubles
Dinner set and ready for her lover
Home he comes food he eats
With a belly that's full shots fired
A bullet in his temple smiles from her face
The rejoicing can go on now
911 call from her,
Her: yes il killed him Come quick,
Operator: Ma'am?
Shot fired
Phone dropped
Another body hit the floor
Silence in room 108

morning craves

your skin is
like the ocean
that il swim in
your eyes are like
the morning sky
that il gawk at
lingering for you
my heart sings
morning praises
of gratefulness
coffee love and pleasure
ah, life's treasure

same ol same

saying you love me
holding you closely
squeezing you tightly
kissing you softly
sit back
relax
unwind
while il explore your mind
you say that he's your man
while he tell the world you're just a friend
so your friends laugh behind your back because they all know the truth
but it sad because everyone know but you
brothers be having permanent cat but be cheating with temporary cat
now here something il don't understand
you guys get a beautiful queen and still fuck up
but it's cool
they pass on the good dudes
for someone like you
turn around be heartbroken
screaming
il hate you
man fuck this
and fuck that
and fuck you too

technology bought my soul:

we tweet away
tweet tweet tweet
before we realize
time has past
we're another year older
we are so drown to our phones
we don't even recognize
the beauty that Mother Earth
has given us
she post a picture on
Instagram for a like
for someone to tell her
she's beautiful
but if she would have
looked up
and noticed nature
she wouldn't need a like
or a comment to tell her she's beautiful
our eyes soaked into
the bright light
that comes from
our cellular device
taking the beauty
from our insight
conversing with our fingers
our vocabulary lacks
nutrients cutting the
words short
letting it say
everything for us
the brown pretty tree
has grown lonely
no one sits underneath
the flowers have sprouted
unnoticed
give your thumb a rest
and workout your tongue

colored love:

her eyes are nothing like the sun
like the tiny blood cells through your needled vein

colors of the morning haze
the pills on your tongue
the room remained numbed
ethereal silence between us

i̶l will split your heart open
and put a amulet in behind the eyes

when the sun is in my eyes
and the atmosphere is calm
i̶l think of you

you're a mixture of books, art, literature, and time

beautiful swelling and delicious aching
what color am i̶l when i̶'m̶l'm naked

insane:

the devil is busy. he ~~fight~~fights my thoughts daily. somehow, he sneaks inside my head and make me feel bad about myself x life. i̶l try to keep my peace, but it seems as if it can all go wrong with the click of a switch. my mind has become a battlefield. good ~~vs~~vs. evil. ~~these the~~these treasures i̶l hide from society, family, x friends. people like you. if you read this, dry your eyes. some days i̶l don't know if i̶l want to live or die. the pain won't go away. hiding under the mask of fear. i̶l believe in God but my faith isn't strong enough i̶l guess.

different views:

these drugs that's in
my veins il cannot feel
the pain you bring

there's some hope
inside this
broken body

we met as
strangers then
we left like strangers

il once knew a girl
who cheated on her man
she thought the grass
was greener on the other side
just as she arrived
it was more damaged
than her last guy

cause the way il see it
nobody's perfect but
if they are worth it
you do whatever

words from a praying man:

but the bones of the hurt
will no longer ache
someday
at least that's what il hope
how could il
let the energy
of another being
take me away from
God's arms
where has my moral gone
to the dead end and back
we said that
a bucket lay next to me
for my tears and sickness
coughing up the love
that you stitched together
each cough loosens
each stitch
il awake to a wet pillow
my sheets are damaged
from my war
that went on through the night
to trust the lips of another
would be hard on thy heart
Lord God
with your angels on my side
your son protecting my back
il ask for your guidance
and remove this illness

a crying mother:

tears falling cause it hurt so much
where there's still love, pain lives
memories of laughter
replays in your thoughts
it's sad to know he called it off
a dagger to the heart
a blessing to the womb
the huge pill to swallow
leading your actions to follow
things won't be the same
what a shame
now you have a seed
that needs ~~it's~~its mommy
but for now, think of your child
let that be your reason to smile

psychotic victim

the darkness that's in this room
somebody else in here with me
(doom doom)
the sounds are coming from my closet
running to see but end up falling
as il reach there, il open the door
nothing was there
the wind from the opened widow
brushed my shoulders
(crash crash)
glasses falling from the cabinet
flying towards the kitchen
nobody there
il felt a tap
heard sounds
here
no over here
grab my gun
then got to bussing
two shots
(pow pow)
now he dead
il hit the lights
now i'mI'm scared
wouldn't you believe
that it was
indeed me
all the time
that was there

voices of the unknown:

but who's to say
the pain you have today
will never go away
and the voices
that you hear
will never be clear

skin:

can il get lost in your garden
where the sun hits
the flowers bloom
where the water is pure
and the birds sing songs of joy
with fresh fruit
that grows from the soil of love
il want to go deep swimming
inside your sea
underneath
where no one has ever been
to a place so warm and dark
our only source of light
is the energy that is being transferred from our bodies
into each other
your body speaks the language of love
and my heart is waiting to be filled

The Book of Haikus:
the birds singing
to the morning light
someone has died

the cold breeze
 brought many things
including her

1:11 am
 winter nights
the flowers shivering

in my bed
lies my shadow
still asleep

the leaves blow
mellow moon
it's quiet

walking in the rain
her skin melts
now we're the same

sound of the night
lovers making out
my what a sight

peaceful library
pot heads
shh!

when the moon sinks
 into the ocean,
sea creatures sing

gawking at the stars
feeling sad,
thinking damn

close your legs
don't open
until Christmas

a falling star
make a wish
oh it's just a raindrop

covered by the clouds,
the sun
sleeps peacefully

~~november~~November
you're just a dream
let us feast

humans, along with memories
we leave scars
sad isn't

~~autumn~~Autumn night in ~~alabama~~Alabama
the southern girl
singing on the bus

a turtle with ~~an~~a head start
the rabbit passes him
the turtle wins

a black ~~jew~~Jew
 and a white hooker
standing together on the corner

a cold wet night
words and crickets
are only up

it's morning
raining, yawning, moaning
somebody's cumming

a blind man

walks into
a dead end
the cloud is grey
my feelings
are blue

woman in red
tight dress
your headlights are on

squeaky bed
the ~~neighbors~~neighbors' voice
next door

~~friday~~Friday night
the two
twenty one year old friends

~~sunday~~Sunday morning
 an aspirin
with a reverend

my poetry notebook knows more
 about you
than it does me

early sun rising
 lust
is in the air

the dog waited
for ~~it's~~its owner
but found a bone instead

a girl
just took a shortcut
through my life

and the fish
 sitting on the boat
out of breath

evening coming

the college girl
unloosing her bra
under the sun
 holds the truth
or lies

winter snow
 the poet
and writer are having coffee

she sleeps naked
 to see if he will come
and still nothing

a full ~~november~~November moon
and yet,
here ~~i~~I am

warm ~~december~~December night
a teenage girl said
"~~i~~I love you" in the dark

3:00 am nights
the sound of
humans breathing

in all black
~~i~~I said a joke
no laughter

white rose with black
  splashes,
cookies & cream ice cream

looking for my heart
 in the garbage
~~i~~I found Mona Lisa

for a moment
   the sun
wore shades

the working boy

he doesn't know
his girl is cheating on him

reading my notes
the fly buzzing from
page to page

~~december~~December in ~~mobile~~Mobile
foggy mornings
 with lots of shopping and robberies

pink moon in ~~november~~November
they hold hands
one last time

it's too dark
to read
your feelings

~~christmas~~Christmas colors
  red and green
on a spring butterfly

two black kids
fighting over a peach soda
on a summer day

secrets to her:

her scent pulled me in
releasing love i've~~I've~~ never felt
the timing late ~~its~~it's after ten
but the soft kisses made me melt
couldn't move a muscle
afraid to end it by pulling away
inside my thoughts wrestle
to see if i~~I~~ was going to stay
inner connecting with each other
sounds of two well needed beings
interacting with one another
expressing their feelings
deep breathing heavy sighs
the voices of pleasure
committing with their eyes
unlocking the treasure
where the human soul detaches itself
we meet at the flesh
hoping to find more than ~~hisself~~his self
to get with her will be a success
let's experience love 101
no need to be scared
though this has never been done
your feelings, i~~I~~ am prepared
driving me insane
let me give you something
that stays in your brain
with your heart erupting
the want to feel your lips
pressed against my skin
as i~~I~~ rub your pierced nips
i~~I~~ move inside and explore within
leaving your body full of life
the oozing from below
as if you were my wife
secrets in your messages, nobody will know
knowing your heart beat for someone else
doesn't mean we must stop here
transfer your energy into myself
i~~I~~ promise to always be there
can we make art
have passionate sex
release my treasure inside your heart
make you forget your ex
my imagination running wild
so can we see if it's true

sad to know it's been awhile
may il change your life and more too

flaws and all:

some may think i'mlI'm perfect
others look at me as nothing
is it the structure of my face
the high cheek bones skinny face
my crooked teeth and deep depression
or the way il look when i'mlI'm dressed
a figure as a pencil hair as a lion
with the skin of cracks and scars
my flaws are so serious that il cannot continue writing this

mad writer

darkness falls upon me
piercing through my soul
that black hole
inside of me

emptying out those hearts of love
in that pile il found my old crush
il was young dumb and in a rush
but God watched me from above

many lonely days
picking at the stale flowers
long hours of hot showers
to wash away my old ways

numbers, words and art
time, energy and flesh
something's just don't mesh
seen it coming from the start

death

woeful soul

it's ~~be~~ been a year since il last saw you
touch your face kissed your lips
nobody knew when this day would come
and we most certainly wasn't expecting this soon
the many laughs we shared
erotic pleasures amongst each other
now the only way to please you is through spirit alone
no longer able to hold your flesh
il connect more with your spirit
leaving me empty in flesh
but full in soul
my mind goes weak at times
pondering on the what if's and how come's
our favorite song played just last week
shall we dance or just go home
my old tears are in a jar with your name on it
saving them for when il go, my people can pour my last tears and il can cry
with them
il was the rock in your waterfalls
here il stand still string holding your ground
you leave me only with memories, love and feelings

remember

remember when you said you will never leave
when you said we'll always be
remember

remember how you told me il was the best to ever do it
how il could never lose it
remember

remember that night we stayed up talking all night
you saying you never want this to end right
remember

remember when you came crying to me
you felt alone and lonely
remember

remember our first huge break up
many tears afterwards but then we'd make up
remember

remember we said forever
here we are not even together
now il know you remember

lonely days

thinking of many ways
to do what ~~il~~ I love
and love what ~~il~~ I do
but maybe life is the tool
and ~~i'm~~ I'm the loose screw
giving to get
instead of giving just because
that may be why ~~i'm~~ I'm so fucked up
~~i've~~ I've had better days
but that's the past and ~~i've~~ I've change my ways
the wise know some days come with loneliness
but create and share
In time you'll get your happiness

lonely fear

with my body
covered in sin
my heart went
on ~~it's~~ its own
and got broken again
the thought of love
brought happiness
to my mind
though it's actions
left me thinking
that ~~i~~ l will never find
the one of a kind
knowing that
~~i~~ l am not perfect
but also knowing
that ~~i~~ l am
far from worthless

Darkness

nyctophilia:

I thought about killing myself a couple of times
but if il told my moms she'll probably lose her fucking mind
hearing this you won't even know it's me
it's weird actually
is suicidal taking the easy way out
life on mute, everything is silent
all il see is trafficking, drug gangs and violence
at first il wouldn't believe it
mental illness has left my thoughts leaking
il close my eyes picturing nothing but dark souls
surrounding my body inside the negative energy flows
my nightmares are becoming realistic
surfing through this time of age where beauty is covered up with plastic
oh this pain, what taste
licking the blood that drips from below my waist
sticking the needle deeper in my veins
just to feel the high that it brings
these memories
those drugs
this pain

to the rape survivors:

il feel your pain
that day your life changed
the fighting and screaming
crying and bleeding
the heavy figure on top
holding you and not a stop
the wetness between you two
what a nasty pleasure upon you
the memory stays there
while the day leaves unfair
silent to the surroundings
wishing you, was instead dying
vision blurry feelings clear
no means no though they didn't care
soon the words you wanted to say
drown underneath that faithful day
as the dark image drains the energy
from your temple you plant ~~an imagery~~imagery
of the moon watching you two
and if the stars feeling for you
a deep sharp pain travels through your lower end
leaving scars that were unwanted
causing you to think again
why me why me
did il do something to deserve this please someone save me
walk around without a soul knowing
but the one who laid on me showing
it's not easy to speak on it
but il felt il needed to say this shit
you may have taken part of me
but you haven't destroyed me
should il not forgive the image that
rested upon my brown skin
or find the inner peace and forgive within
to be sexually abuse by someone you trusted
and what makes it worse knowing that they're loving it
this is not a joke and this isn't just for me
il pray that someday this raping comes to a cease
il wrote this poem because il too
was rape not by one but by two
so when il say il feel you il feel you

rape is a serious situation and to anyone who has or goes through it, il pray you
overcome it. il love you and not just physically but mentally.

Made in the USA
San Bernardino, CA
09 February 2015